Why Can't a Man Be More Like a Cat?

*Notes, observations, and
ruminations providing
paws for thought*

Linda Konner AND
Antonia van der Meer

ILLUSTRATIONS BY
Adrienne Hartman

Why Can't a Man Be More Like a Cat?

Robson Books

First published in Great Britain in 1996 by Robson Books Ltd,
Bolsover House, 5-6 Clipstone Street, London W1P 8LE

Second impression 1996
Third impression 1997
Fourth impression 1998

Copyright © 1995 by Linda Konner and Antonia van der Meer
Illustrations copyright © 1995 by Adrienne Hartman
The right of Linda Konner and Antonia van der Meer to be identified
as authors of this work has been asserted by them in accordance with
the Copyright, Designs and Patents Act 1988

British Library Cataloguing in Publication Data
A catalogue record for this title is available from the British Library

ISBN 1 86105 060 7

Printed by The Guernsey Press Company Limited, Guernsey,
Channel Islands

To all the cats
we've ever loved before
and to the two Peters
we love now

When a cat comes in at 2:00 A.M., he doesn't wake you up by crashing into the furniture.

Cats don't have to be called twice for dinner.

Cats wash their own plates.

Cats don't wear smelly socks.

Cats don't care if you cheat at Monopoly.

Cats have soft whiskers.

$\mathcal{C}$ats like to snuggle.

$\mathcal{C}$ats like all the same TV shows you do.

$\mathcal{C}$ats never want to rent *Hollywood Chainsaw Hookers*.

$\mathcal{C}$ats understand your moods.

When a cat takes a nap on your couch, there's still room for you.

$\mathcal{C}$ats agree that home is the nicest place to be.

$\mathcal{Y}$ou'll never find out that your cat is married to someone else.

$\mathcal{C}$ats can't borrow money from you.

$\mathcal{C}$ats don't think it's politically incorrect to wear fur.

A cat won't come back from the barbershop with a goofy haircut.

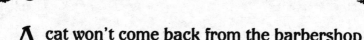

C ats lick their own body parts.

C ats don't steal the blankets.

A cat's hairline will never recede.

C ats don't care how long it's been since you last shaved your legs.

Cats never flush the toilet while you're taking a shower.

Cats don't wear stupid hats with team logos.

Cats aren't embarrassed by the Tampax box in your bathroom.

Cats never have to have the last word.

C ats don't need as much stroking.

C ats don't use the remote control to watch thirty-four shows at once.

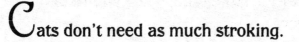

C ats may stray but they always come home to you.

W hen you're traveling with cats, they don't think it's a crime to stop and ask for directions.

Cats keep their opinions to themselves.

*C*ats never claim they know how to fix large appliances.

Cats are never threatened when you make more money than they do.

Your cat won't run off with the baby-sitter.

Cats love your legs (at least brushing up against them).

Cats don't leave the toilet seat up.

Cats love heavy petting.

Cats understand the fine art of just hanging around.

Cats never shout.

Cats think a Super Bowl is simply a bigger dish for their food.

Cats don't tell you to get off the phone.

Cats don't criticize your mother.

Cats have nine lives.

Cats don't rip articles out of the newspaper before you've had a chance to read it.

When a cat joins you in the bathroom, there's still room to breathe.

A cat doesn't spend hours in front of the mirror checking his hairline.

When cats have bad dreams, they don't wake you up in the middle of the night to tell you about them.

Cats don't whine about being neutered.

Cats never question how much you're eating.

Cats are less afraid of the vacuum cleaner.

Cats don't make calls to sex lines.

Cats don't make dumb excuses when they come home after a night on the prowl.

Chubby cats are cute.

Cats always land on their feet.

Cats don't ask who was on the phone.

Cats stay the whole night.

Cats don't use your toothbrush.

C ats understand the importance of beauty sleep.

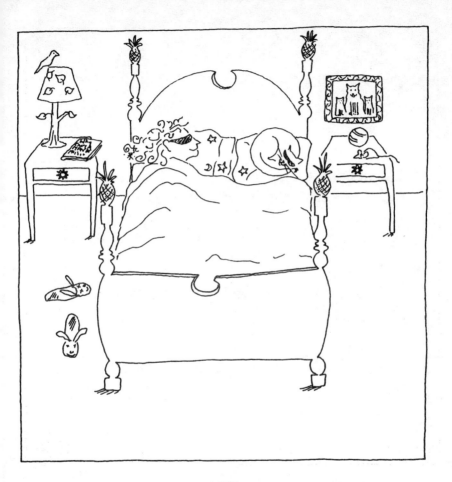

*C*ats don't leave their toenail clippings on the floor.

*C*ats don't laugh at you for crying through *Gone With the Wind* on video.

*C*ats aren't interested in your measurements.

*C*ats don't spend the whole weekend watching sports on TV.

A cat's nose is never too big for his face.

C ats won't compare your food unfavorably with Mom's.

C ats will hang around with you even when you have PMS.

C ats never have a bad hair day.

Cats know when to stop eating.

C ats don't keep change in mayonnaise jars on the dresser.

C ats don't misplace things and then blame it on you.

A cat doesn't need to be reassured constantly that the boss likes him.

C ats don't leave crumbs.

Cats don't leave wet towels on the floor.

Cats don't snore.

Cats don't drink milk out of the container (then put it back in the refrigerator with two drops left).

Cats don't smoke cigars.

C ats know that every mess holds creative possibilities.

Cats don't say, "Are you gaining weight?"

Cats don't say, "Why didn't you wake me up?"

Cats don't leave hair on the soap.

Cats don't crack their knuckles.

C ats don't complain when the MasterCard bill comes.

C ats don't start a conversation with you while you're brushing your teeth.

C ats don't steam up the bathroom mirror.

C ats don't leave their whiskers all over the bathroom sink.

Cats don't interrupt.

C ats don't leave big shoes in the middle of the
floor for you to trip over.

A cat doesn't wear toilet paper on his face.

Cats say "I love you" in creative ways.

Cats don't snap the window shades up while you're still half-dressed.

Cats don't tell you to keep the kids quiet.

Cats don't obsess over their cholesterol level.

Cats don't imply that all the kids' bad traits were inherited from you.

Cats never look their age.

Cats don't think you're a wimp if you ask them to catch a mouse for you.

Cats love laundry day.

C ats don't always have an ulterior motive when they rub up against you.

C ats can find you in the dark.

C ats won't look up from their dinner and announce, "This tastes like dog food."

C ats don't run up enormous bills in hardware stores.

Cats don't expect you to read the map.

Cats don't wear socks with sandals.

You'll never find out that your live-in cat is really gay.

Cats never think they're having a heart attack.

Cats are happy to let you drive.

*C*ats never say, "Are you having your period?"

*C*ats never need a shave.

*C*ats never say, "I just want to hear the score."

*C*ats don't hog the bathroom.

Cats don't work late.

Cats don't set the alarm for 5:00 A.M. and expect you to sleep through it.

Cats don't change your soft-rock radio station to the all-news station for traffic reports.

Cats don't turn the air conditioner to the Freeze setting.

C ats don't think you need to get more exercise.

C ats know a ball of yarn is much more fun than a baseball.

When you say the word "diamond," cats don't immediately think of baseball.

Cats have cute little feet.

Cats enjoy a little foreplay before they pounce on their prey.

Cats don't fool around with anything stronger than catnip.

Cats never say they'll call and then don't.

Cats don't like dogs better.

Cats don't give a second glance to your beautiful friend when she comes over to dinner.

Cats accept canned food.

A cat would never mount another animal's head on the wall.

Cats don't ignore you at parties.

Cats are comforting.

A cat can get from the windowsill to the top of the refrigerator in a single bound.

The hair sticking out of a cat's ears is cute.

A cat's long silences are soothing, not upsetting.

C ats don't bring up the names of their former girlfriends.

W hen cats get sick, they do it quietly.

C ats don't get upset if you invite people to dinner when Monday night football is on.

Cats don't wear plaid.

Cats don't mind dancing with you.

Cats don't walk off with the one section of the Sunday paper you were just about to read.

Cats won't get mad if you eat the last of the ice cream.

Cats don't say anything about how you look when you wake up in the morning.

Cats aren't car crazy.

Cats don't brag about their endurance.

Cats never make fun of what you say.

Cats never ask, "Walk much?" when you stumble while wearing your three-inch heels.

C ats understand that furniture needs to be replaced every now and then.

Cats never have tantrums.

Cats don't think it's amusing party behavior to stick a straw up their left nostril.

Cats don't whine when you go out and leave them home alone.

Cats don't get athlete's foot.

Cats didn't descend from the apes.

Cats don't worry about how you'll pay for things.

Cats never have an identity crisis.

Cats don't care whether your bra unhooks from the back or the front.

C ats pick better hiding places.

C ats don't carp if you forget to pay the electric bill.

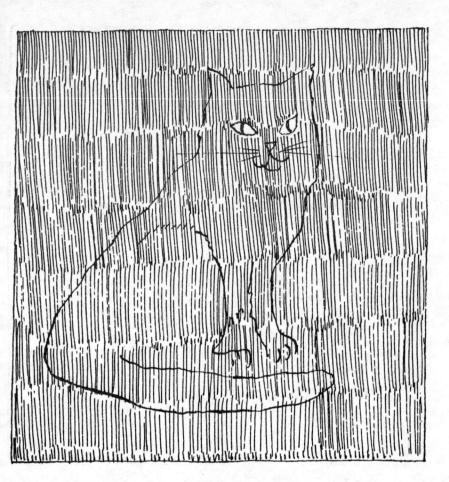

Cats know when to be quiet.

Your cat won't leave you to join the navy.

Cats have fewer germs than men.

Cats don't have tattoos.

Cats aren't annoyed by the stuffed animals all over your bed.

Cats don't give you a hard time if you want to read in bed.

Cats can make the commitment.

Cats don't equate speed with sexual prowess.

C ats don't complain when you get a short haircut.

Cats don't talk about financial planning over dinner.

Cats don't wonder what you do all day.

Cats don't cause a tidal wave when they lie down on your water bed.

A cat will never treat you like a dog.

When cats get the seven-year itch, all they do is scratch it.

A cat doesn't expect you to be the one to remember his mother's birthday.

Cats agree that the only good mouse is a dead mouse.

Cats don't desire big, expensive toys (like Lamborghinis, power saws, and oversize stereo systems).

C ats maintain their appearance even on weekends.

~ 91 ~

When your cat sneezes, your china doesn't rattle in the cupboard.

Your downstairs neighbors never complain about your cat's heavy footsteps.

Purring is much nicer to listen to than snoring.

You can put a bell on your cat and know where he is at all times.

Cats don't get beer bellies.

Cats don't expect you to be sympathetic to their every mood.

Cats believe that Cat Woman makes an excellent role model.

A cat's little love bites heal faster.

One good purr can be worth a thousand words.

C ats always look good first thing in the morning.

$\mathcal{C}$ats can take care of themselves.

$\mathcal{C}$ats are trustworthy.

$\mathcal{C}$ ats never finish a meal with food stuck to their faces.

$\mathcal{C}$ ats are able to remain mysterious throughout the years.

Cats have the good sense to stay out of the rain.

Cats never recoil in horror when you accidentally cough near them.

Cats keep all your secrets.

Cats will never accuse you of being catty.

Cats let sleeping dogs lie.

Cats wake you with a kiss.

Cats know what to do about spilt milk.

Cats are affectionate.

Cats are discriminating.

C ats won't look at you seriously and say, "We have to talk."

C ats won't come home one day with a brand-new puppy and say, "Isn't he cute?"

C ats are interested in your opinions.

A cat won't give the waiter his order before you've even opened your menu.

C ats aren't afraid to open themselves up to you.

C ats know exactly what girlie magazines are good for.

C ats aren't turned off by public displays of affection.

C ats come when you call them (or at least when they hear the sound of the can opener).

C ats don't try to rush you when you're putting on your makeup.

C ats don't mind if you're flat chested.

Cats wash themselves every day.

Cats won't leave you for a teenager after you've been together for a long time.

Cats can slip in through the window.

Cats don't lie to you.

Cats don't slam the screen door.

Cats never yell, "We're out of toilet paper!"

Cats never tell you how to handle your boss.

Cats don't endlessly comparison-shop for stereo equipment.

Cats are patient.

If your cat doesn't want to go for his annual checkup, you can just stuff him in a box and take him there.

Cats don't own little black books.

Cats take time to stop and smell the roses.

Cats don't need to suck in their stomachs when they walk by a mirror.

Cats ignore your faults.

Cats are good listeners.

Cats don't care if you eat all the red M&M's.

A cat will get up off his chair to greet you when you come home.

Cats look up to you.

Cats don't try to squeeze into their college clothes.

Cats are willing to share a sleeping bag with you.

Cats know when to get out of the kitchen.

Cats don't fantasize about quitting the rat race to live off the land in the Maine wilderness.

Cats don't expect you to change your name.

Cats never wake up with a hangover.

Cats don't wonder why it takes you so long to get dressed in the morning.

*C*ats don't yell at you for leaving the hallway lights on all night.

*C*ats never steal the last piece of cake.

*C*ats don't ask you to sign complicated legal papers before they move in with you.

*C*ats don't use up all the hot water.

~ 121 ~

C ats don't need to wear goofy rubber waders just to catch a few fish.

Cats always cover their tracks.

Cats don't ask you what you're doing when you're just sitting there on the couch.

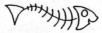

Cats don't accidentally lock themselves out of the house.

Cats don't care if the scale is a few pounds off (in your favor).

When you bring in the mail, none of it is for your cat.

Cats take hair loss in stride.

Cats aren't party animals.

Cats don't drink to excess.

Cats are worthy of worship.

Cats aren't allergic to cats.

Cats don't read the paper the whole time you're cleaning the kitchen, giving the dog a flea bath, and putting the kids to bed.

Cats never get hung up about who's top dog.

Cats don't always need to be right.

Cats aren't ashamed to let you hear them cry.

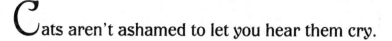

Cats don't care if you were too tired to do the ironing.

Cats don't talk about moving to Florida when the weather turns cold.

Cats don't keep telling you your jokes aren't funny.

Cats happily take it on the chin.

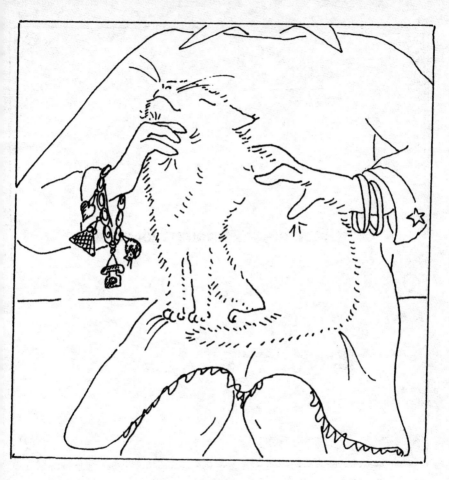

Cats love when you go shopping.

*C*ats are always down-to-earth.

*C*ats don't fill the attic with useless college mementos.

*C*ats don't complain about finding cat hair on everything.

*C*ats don't get nervous when you watch the Home Shopping Network.

C ats like it when you wear your comfortable old flannel nightgown to bed.

A cat living in the White House always manages to stay high in the opinion polls.

C ats don't kiss and tell.

C ats can't read your private journal.

Cats like to play footsie.

Cats never return the gifts you get them.

~ 138 ~

Cats don't care if you clean the house as long as you clean the litter box.

Cats don't undress you with their eyes.

Cats don't think they're funnier than late-night talk show hosts.

C ats don't have to pay half their income in kitty support.

C ats don't play golf.

W hen cats claw their way to the top, they don't really hurt anyone.

Cats are able to keep the romance alive.

~ 143 ~